VENUS

MURRAY "OAK" TAPETA

OUTER SPACE

NORWOOD HOUSE PRESS

Cataloging-in-Publication Data

Names: Tapeta, Murray.
Title: Venus / Murray Tapeta.
Description: Buffalo, NY : Norwood House Press, 2026. | Series: Outer space | Includes glossary and index.
Identifiers: ISBN 9781978574984 (pbk.) | ISBN 9781978574991 (library bound) | ISBN 9781978575004 (ebook)
Subjects: Venus (Planet)--Juvenile literature.
Classification: LCC QB621.T374 2026 | DDC 523.42--dc23

Published in 2026 by
Norwood House Press
2544 Clinton Street
Buffalo, NY 14224

Copyright © 2026 Norwood House Press
Designer: Rhea Magaro
Editor: Kim Thompson

Photo credits: Cover, p. 1, 14 Artsiom P/Shutterstock.com; pp. 5, 6, 9, 17 NASA Images; p. 7 Vladi333/Shutterstock.cover; p. 8 Feng Cheng/Shutterstock.com; pp. 10, 11 Aphelleon/Shutterstock.com; p. 13 ra3rn; p. 15 3445128471/Shutterstock.com; p. 16 Jurik Peter/Shutterstock.com; p. 18 Elenarts/Shutterstock.com; p. 19 Raymond Cassel/Shutterstock.com; p. 21 Jne Valokuvaus/Shutterstock.com;

All rights reserved. No part of this book may be reproduced in any form without permission in writing from the publisher, except by a reviewer.

Printed in the United States of America

Some of the images in this book illustrate individuals who are models. The depictions do not imply actual situations or events.

CPSIA compliance information: Batch #CSNHP26: For further information contact Norwood House Press at 1-800-237-9932.

TABLE OF CONTENTS

Where Is Venus?..4

How Was Venus Discovered? 8

What Is It Like on Venus? 10

Has Venus Been Explored? 18

Glossary 22

Thinking Questions 23

Index 24

About the Author 24

Where Is Venus?

Our **solar system** has eight planets. Venus is the second planet from the Sun. It is about the same size as Earth. Venus is the brightest object in Earth's night sky other than the moon.

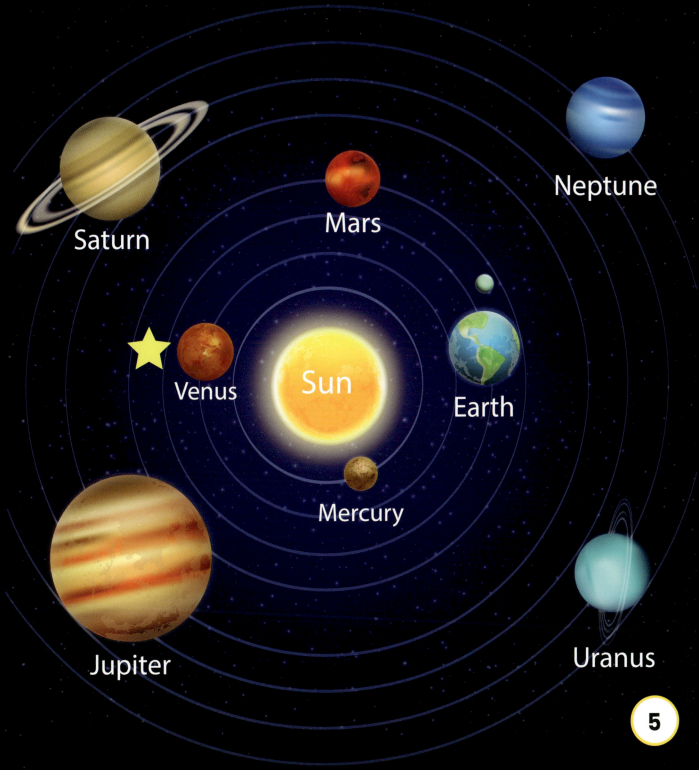

Venus is over 67 million miles (108 million kilometers) from the Sun. Traveling from Earth to Venus would take over a month.

One year on Venus is 225 Earth days long. It takes Venus that long to **orbit** the Sun.

How Was Venus Discovered?

Ancient people noticed bright Venus. They named the planet after the Roman goddess of love and beauty.

From Earth, Venus shines brightest just before sunrise and just after sunset. Venus is often called "the morning star" or "the evening star."

The Italian **astronomer** Galileo Galilei first saw Venus through a **telescope** in 1610.

What Is It Like on Venus?

Venus is a **terrestrial** planet. Its surface is rocky. It has thousands of volcanoes.

Venus does not have a moon. An **asteroid** orbits the planet. Scientists have named it Zoozve.

Gravity on Venus is about the same as on Earth. If you weighed 100 pounds (45 kilograms) on Earth, you would weigh 91 pounds (41 kilograms) on Venus.

13

Venus has a thick **atmosphere**. It traps the Sun's heat. Venus is the hottest planet in our solar system.

Winds can blow 224 miles (360 kilometers) per hour. There are yellow clouds made of sulfuric acid. Hot sulfuric acid smells like rotten eggs. Venus is a stinky planet!

Scientists believe Venus formed nearly five billion years ago. It began as a swirling disk of gas and dust. Over time, it became a planet.

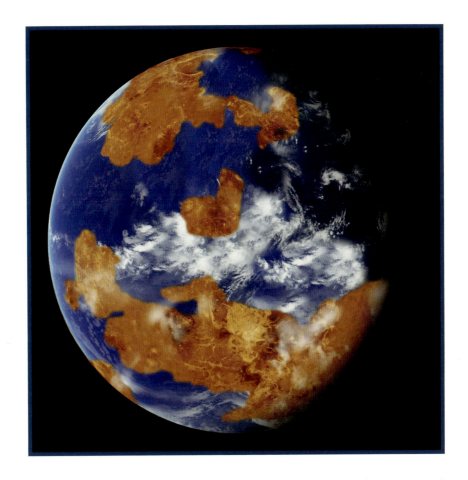

People could not live on Venus. It is too hot and stormy. But long ago, Venus may have been more like Earth. Its climate may have changed over time.

Has Venus Been Explored?

Venus is one of the most explored planets. Over 40 spacecrafts and **satellites** have been sent there to collect data.

A few spacecrafts have landed on Venus. Some sent back photos. None of them worked for more than two hours.

Scientists will continue to study "Earth's twin," Venus. They want to know more about our solar system's brightest planet.

Glossary

asteroid (AS-tuh-roid): a small rocky object that orbits a planet or the Sun; an object in space made from leftover material from when the solar system formed

astronomer (uh-STRAH-nuh-mer): a scientist who studies objects in the sky, including planets, galaxies, and stars

atmosphere (AT-muhs-feer): the mixture of gases that surrounds a planet; air

gravity (GRAV-i-tee): an invisible force that pulls objects toward each other and keeps them from floating away

orbit (OR-bit): to follow a curved path around a larger body in space

satellites (SAT-uh-lites): spacecrafts sent into orbit around a planet, moon, or other object in space

solar system (SOH-lur SIS-tuhm): the Sun and everything that orbits around it

telescope (TEL-uh-skope): an instrument that helps people see distant objects

terrestrial (tuh-RES-tree-uhl): made up of rocks or metals and having a hard surface

Thinking Questions

1. How did Venus get its name?

2. Describe the climate on Venus.

3. Which is longer: a Venus year or an Earth year? Why?

4. Why do you think Venus is called "Earth's twin"?

5. Why do you think it is difficult for spacecrafts to survive on the surface of Venus?

Index

asteroid 11

astronomer 9

atmosphere 14

Earth 4, 6, 8, 12, 17, 20

Galilei, Galileo 9

gravity 12

orbit 7, 11

Sun 4, 6, 7, 14

volcanoes 10

winds 15

About the Author

Murray "Oak" Tapeta was born in a cabin without plumbing in Montana. Growing up in the great outdoors, he became a lover of nature. He earned the nickname "Oak" after climbing to the top of an oak tree at the age of three. Oak loves to read and write. He has written many books about events in history and other subjects that fascinate him. He prefers spending time in the wilderness with his dog Birchy.